The Trinket

Written and illustrated by Nicola Senior

Collins

The Treetop Club went to visit the pond.
The soft brown mud had a damp smell.

Frank spotted a bright thing glinting in the sunlight. An object was sparkling in the moist pondweed.

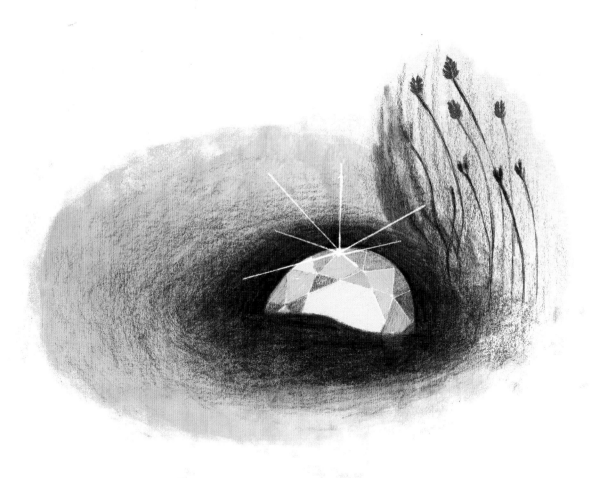

Frank thrust in his hand and got it free. The object was sparkling like frost and starlight.

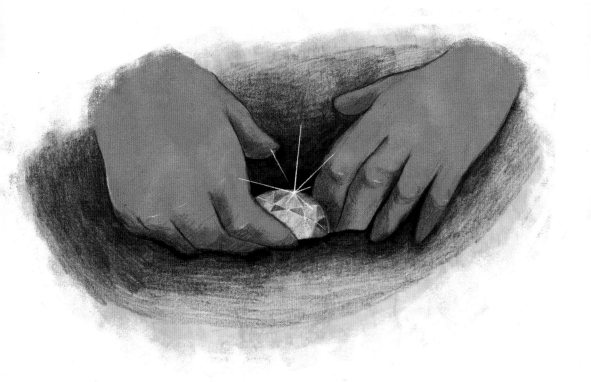

Frank and the Treetop Club trooped back.

What do you think this is?

"Look, Mum!" said Frank, dropping it in the sink with a sploosh. They cleared the clumps of mud from it.

"I think it is a trinket from a crown," Mum said.

"Or the cloak of a wizard," said Frank.

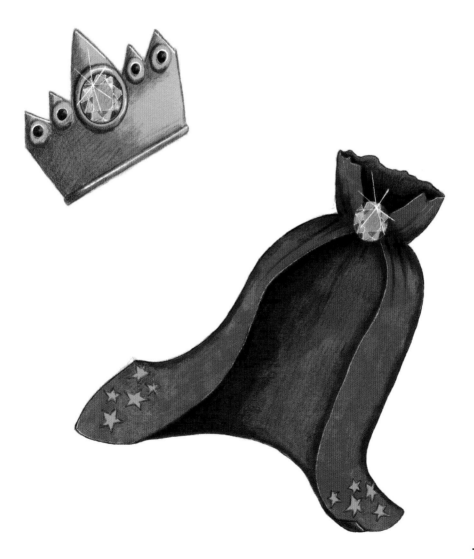

Frank got the Treetop Club to meet in the camp.

"We must look for the person that has lost the trinket," said Frank. They all agreed.

They pinned banners on the tree trunks near the pond.

Have you lost something?

We might have it!

But no one claimed the trinket.
Frank took the banners down.

Then Frank spotted his gran, sitting on the bench. She looked distressed.

"What is the matter?" said Frank.

"The sparkling part of my ring is lost," she explained.

"We have it!" Frank exclaimed.

Gran was thrilled to have
the trinket back.

13

The trinket

Review: After reading

Use your assessment from hearing the children read to choose any GPCs, words or tricky words that need additional practice.

Read 1: Decoding

- Challenge the children, working in pairs, to come up with a similar word or phrase that could be swapped for these without changing the meaning of the sentence:

  page 6 **sploosh** (e.g. *splash, splosh*) page 10 **gathered** (e.g. *grew, appeared*)

  page 6 **cleared** (e.g. *cleaned off, removed*) page 13 **thrilled** (e.g. *delighted, excited*)

- Ask the children to sound out and read the following words. Remind them to break longer words into chunks or syllables if necessary:

  glint/ing   **ex/plained**   **star/light**

  scoot/er   **ex/claimed**

- Ask the children to take turns to read a sentence of the story. Say: Can you blend in your head when you read the words?

Read 2: Prosody

- Turn to pages 8 and 9 and focus on the punctuation.

- On page 8, demonstrate reading the second sentence without pausing at the comma. Ask: Have I read that correctly? If necessary, reread the sentence with a pause and point out how the comma separates the spoken words from **said Frank**.

- On page 9, ask the children to read the notice on the tree. Say: Look out for the punctuation, as this will affect how you read the two sentences. If necessary, revise a questioning tone and discuss the appropriate tone for the exclamation.

Read 3: Comprehension

- Ask the children if they have ever found something in the ground, or read another book about something being found in the ground. Talk about buried treasures.

- Focus the children on pages 12 and 13. Ask: Why was Gran sad? (*she lost the jewel from her ring*) What made her happy? (*Frank found it*) Talk about the theme of "lost and found", and how losing things can be upsetting.

- Ask: What is the trinket in the story? (*The sparkling part of Gran's ring*) Discuss how the word trinket tells us that this ring has a jewel in it that is not expensive but is meaningful to gran. Ask the children: What other things do they think could be a trinket?

- Look at pages 14 and 15, and encourage the children to use the pictures to help them retell the story in the correct sequence.